Summary and Analysis of

HELTER SKELTER

The True Story of the Manson Murders

Based on the Book by Vincent Bugliosi

WORTH BOOKS
SMART SUMMARIES

All rights reserved, including without limitation the right to reproduce this book or any portion thereof in any form or by any means, whether electronic or mechanical, now known or hereinafter invented, without the express written permission of the publisher.

This Worth Books book is based on the 2001 paperback edition of *Helter Skelter* by Vincent Bugliosi with Curt Gentry published by W. W. Norton.

Summary and analysis copyright © 2017 by Open Road Integrated Media, Inc.

ISBN: 978-1-5040-4672-5

Worth Books
180 Maiden Lane
Suite 8A
New York, NY 10038
www.worthbooks.com

Worth Books is a division of Open Road Integrated Media, Inc.

The summary and analysis in this book are meant to complement your reading experience and bring you closer to a great work of nonfiction. This book is not intended as a substitute for the work that it summarizes and analyzes, and it is not authorized, approved, licensed, or endorsed by the work's author or publisher. Worth Books makes no representations or warranties with respect to the accuracy or completeness of the contents of this book.

Contents

Context	1
Overview	5
Summary	9
Timeline	25
Cast of Characters	29
Direct Quotes and Analysis	39
Trivia	43
What's That Word?	47
Critical Response	49
About the Authors	51
For Your Information	53
Bibliography	55

Context

Vincent Bugliosi published *Helter Skelter: The True Story of the Manson Murders* in 1974, three years after the conviction of the Manson "Family." The nine murders they committed were a major news story, and Bugliosi—a lead prosecutor—had become a celebrity in his own right. The book was an instant bestseller. Bugliosi's insider perspective of the crimes, investigation, and trial were in high demand, and *Helter Skelter* set the standard for the true-crime genre.

The Manson Family's depravity is often seen as the symbolic end of the freewheeling decadence of the 1960s, the inevitable crash after a decade-long party. Charles Manson was a petty con man and drifter until he moved to San Francisco's Haight-Ashbury

SUMMARY AND ANALYSIS

neighborhood in 1967, where he observed the hippie culture and began picking up followers, mostly teenage runaways and prostitutes. Many hippies lived in "communes," or communal living spaces centered around a quasi-socialist ideology of sharing work and resources. Charlie and his early disciples established their base at Spahn Ranch, an old movie set for Westerns in the Simi Hills of Los Angeles.

As the Manson Family grew closer, Charlie used his charisma and political rhetoric to indoctrinate his followers, ultimately convincing them to fulfill his diabolical plan of instigating a race war through murder. The fame of the victims made the murders even more shocking: Sharon Tate, a well-known actress married to director Roman Polanski who was pregnant with his child; heiress Abigail Folger (of Folgers Coffee) and her boyfriend; and Jay Sebring, a hairdresser to the stars in Hollywood. Furthermore, Dennis Wilson, the drummer of the Beach Boys, had spent time with Manson and the Family.

The murders committed by the Manson Family would have interesting reverberations just around the historical corner. Patty Hearst was abducted in 1974, three years after the Family's convictions, and in 1978, cult leader Jim Jones of the Peoples Temple convinced more than nine hundred of his followers to drink poison. These events shaped our current understanding of brainwashing and cult mentality.

HELTER SKELTER

Where are they now? Charles Manson remains in prison, as do most of the other Family members. In 2014, it was reported that Manson was engaged to a twenty-six-year-old woman, although the relationship fizzled out. He is up for parole in 2027, when he will be ninety-two. Family member Lynette "Squeaky" Fromme was paroled from prison in 2009 after serving time for the attempted assassination of President Gerald Ford. Susan Atkins died in prison that same year.

Overview

The 1969 murders of actress Sharon Tate—pregnant wife of director Roman Polanski—and her friends Abigail Folger, Voytek Frykowski, and Jay Sebring (along with a young man visiting the property's caretaker), shocked the city of Los Angeles for their senselessness and brutality. The victims were beaten, shot, and stabbed numerous times and the word "pig" was written on the front door in blood. The very next day brought news of another shocking crime: the murders of grocery store owner Leno LaBianca and his wife, Rosemary, both also stabbed repeatedly. The words "healter skelter [*sic*]" were written in blood on the LaBiancas' refrigerator.

Different jurisdictions scramble to piece together information, but a break in the case comes when sev-

SUMMARY AND ANALYSIS

eral witnesses agree to talk. While conducting raids for unrelated crimes on two ranches in the desert, police uncover members of the "Manson Family"—a cultish hippie commune devoted to a charismatic con man, Charles Manson. One member, seeking escape, points police to Susan Atkins, who had bragged about being involved with another murder. When Atkins is arrested and imprisoned, she tells her cellmates about being present at the Tate residence as well. Two motorcycle gang members name Manson as the group's leader and assert that he boasted to them about several murders.

Another "Family" member, Leslie Van Houten, implicates herself and Linda Kasabian. Seeking a lighter sentence, Susan Atkins tells a grand jury all about the Tate and LaBianca murders in horrifying detail, pointing the finger at Manson, Van Houten, Kasabian, Charles "Tex" Watson, and Patricia Krenwinkel. Fingerprints found at the Tate scene match Watson and Krenwinkel. The grand jury indicts Van Houten, Manson, Watson, Krenwinkel, Atkins, and Kasabian.

Current and former Family members also provide the investigators with a motive: Manson believed that if he could convince authorities that Black Panthers had committed the murders, a race war (which he called "helter skelter") would ensue. While "the blacks" would win this war, they would find themselves incapable of taking over and ruling American society, and Manson and the Family would step in.

Manson convinces Susan Atkins to recant and Linda Kasabian becomes the prosecution's star witness. Kasabian and a number of other former Family associates testify about the murders and Manson's confessions. Atkins, Krenwinkel, and Van Houten confess in a bid to save Manson. The jury sees through the ruse and reaches a guilty verdict for all parties. The death penalty is doled out, but all of the sentences are commuted to life imprisonment when the California Supreme Court abolishes capital punishment.

Summary

Part 1

The scene is 10050 Cielo Drive in Los Angeles, the residence of director Roman Polanski and his pregnant wife, actress Sharon Tate. On the morning of August 10, 1969, the Polanskis' housekeeper, Winifred Chapman, arrives to discover a cut phone line and, once inside the gate, two bodies on the lawn and another in a vehicle parked in the driveway. These were Abigail Folger, heiress to the Folger Coffee fortune; Voytek Frykowski, her boyfriend; and Steve Parent, a friend of William Garretson, the caretaker living in the guest house.

SUMMARY AND ANALYSIS

When police arrive and enter the home, they find the bodies of Tate and her ex-boyfriend, Hollywood hairdresser Jay Sebring, along with marijuana, methamphetamines, and the word "pig" written in blood on the door. The murders were savage; the victims had been beaten, shot, and stabbed repeatedly. There is wild speculation by police and the press, suggesting a drug-fueled party, orgy, or ritual sacrifice gone awry. William Garretson is an obvious suspect, being the only person left alive on the premises, but he is ruled out after a polygraph test.

In a house across town the next night, teenager Frank Struthers returns home from a camping trip to find all of the curtains drawn. Sensing that this is unusual, he calls his sister. The two of them, along with the sister's boyfriend, enter the house and discover the bodies of their parents, Leno and Rosemary LaBianca, both of whom had been brutally stabbed, choked, and beaten. The word "war" is carved into Leno LaBianca's stomach, the words "healter skelter [*sic*]" are written on the refrigerator in blood. Though Manson knew someone who lived in the LaBianca's neighborhood, their house was chosen completely at random.

A sergeant from the Sherriff's Department alerts the Los Angeles Police Department to similarities in the Tate case and another recent murder: that of music teacher Gary Hinman, where the words "political piggy" had been written in blood. This information is ignored. The similarities between the Tate and LaBianca cases are also disregarded. The LAPD circulates fliers seeking the gun used in the murders, unaware that it is already sitting in a precinct evidence locker in Van Nuys, having been found by a child in Sherman Oaks and turned over to police. Complicating matters further is a rivalry between investigators assigned to the Tate case and those assigned to the LaBianca case. The former are "old guard," the latter, "young upstarts" who are more willing to think outside the box.

About a week after the murders, police arrest twenty-six members of a hippie commune located at Spahn Ranch in the San Fernando Valley for auto theft. Spahn Ranch was an abandoned movie set created for Hollywood Westerns, whose owner, George Spahn, was allowing the hippies to squat there in exchange for labor and female companionship. After he visited, Bugliosi described it as "a very strange place."

Part 2

Investigators working on the LaBianca case finally check in with the Sheriff's Department and learn more about the murder of Gary Hinman. The Sheriff's Department raids Barker Ranch in Death Val-

SUMMARY AND ANALYSIS

ley, a nearly inaccessible enclave in the desert surrounded by rocky terrain, where the aforementioned hippie commune members, released on bail, had fled. Twenty-four arrests are made.

These hippies are members of the "Manson Family," named after their leader, Charles Manson. Manson had conned his followers into believing he was a messiah or Christ figure, preyed on their weaknesses, and made them completely dependent on him. Many were female teen runaways or prostitutes with nowhere else to go. Manson used many methods to control his disciples, from threats, to flattery, to drugs and sex. He had a grifter's natural ability to spot weakness in people and exploit it.

During the raid on Barker Ranch, one Manson Family member, Susan Atkins, is implicated by another in the Hinman murder.

Upon being remanded to jail, Susan Atkins tells fellow inmate Ronnie Howard about being present for the Tate murders. Howard informs the police. At the same time, LaBianca detectives interview Al Springer and Danny DeCarlo, members of a motorcycle gang who had visited Spahn Ranch and heard details about the Tate and LaBianca murders, and other crimes, from Charles Manson.

DeCarlo implicates several other Family members, including Tex Watson and Steve Grogan (a.k.a. "Clem Tufts"), and provides the motive: Manson was hoping to pin the murders on the Black Panthers and instigate a race war. Faced with a multitude of crimes, confessions, and aliases, it becomes increasingly difficult for investigators to piece together identities and the actual order of events.

Part 3

Vincent Bugliosi is assigned as prosecutor and begins his own investigation, visiting Spahn and Barker Ranch to collect evidence. He outlines the raid that had occurred in October of 1969, naming Family members Leslie Van Houten, Patricia Krenwinkel, "Clem Tufts," and Manson himself as four of the people arrested at Barker.

Bugliosi and coauthor Curt Gentry provide a lengthy bio and criminal history of Manson, born Charles Milles Maddox. As an "illegitimate" child of a sixteen-year-old mother, Manson spent his youth in and out of correctional institutions, committing his first armed robbery at age thirteen. This was followed by charges of grand theft auto, rape, pimping, and forgery. In prison, he became very interested in Scientology and the Beatles and began playing music himself. Upon release his in 1967, he relocated to San Francisco and started swindling wayward youths into giving him money, sex, and their total devotion.

SUMMARY AND ANALYSIS

Susan Atkins is offered a plea deal for providing information. Leslie Van Houten corroborates what she can of Atkins's story about the murders and implicates Linda Kasabian, who turns herself in to authorities, claiming innocence.

Meanwhile, police find a match for a fingerprint left on the front door of the Tate house: Tex Watson. Another print belongs to Patricia Krenwinkel. Susan Atkins provides chilling testimony to the grand jury, relating details of the murders. She names Manson, Van Houten, Kasabian, and Krenwinkel in the murders of the LaBiancas. It is noted that she exhibits no "remorse, sorrow, or guilt." The grand jury comes back with indictments for Manson, Watson, Krenwinkel, Van Houten, Atkins, and Kasabian. Manson insists he will represent himself at trial.

Police finally track down the Family's gun, which has been in the Van Nuys precinct since September of that year.

Part 4

Vincent Bugliosi and the other investigators try to pinpoint Manson and the Family's motives. Several witnesses (including Atkins) outline Manson's intention to start a race war (a.k.a. "helter skelter") by blaming the Black Panthers for the murders. According to Manson, after "the black man" won this war, he would find himself ill-equipped to rule society and seek out Charlie and the Family (who had been hiding safely in a "bottomless pit" in Death Valley) to take over.

Manson believed this prophecy was backed up by quotations from the Bible's Book of Revelations and, more peculiarly, references made by the Beatles in various songs from *The White Album*. Charlie felt that the Beatles lyrics were "direct communications to him." Furthermore, several of the songs contained words or phrases written in blood at the murder scenes: "pig," "rise," and "he[a]lter skelter."

Former Family member Paul Watkins tells investigators about Manson's techniques for domination and manipulation, which include rationing out food and drugs, threatening violence, and demanding sex acts.

Bugliosi discovers a link between Manson and the house at 10050 Cielo Drive. Manson had been to the house before the murders, seeking record producer Terry Melcher. According to members of the Family, Melcher had promised to produce an album for Charlie and then changed his mind. While Charlie knew Melcher no longer lived at the address, it would have held a certain symbolic appeal to launch "helter skelter" from this location because he associated it with Melcher's betrayal.

Manson continues to exert influence from his prison cell, using members of the Family who aren't in custody to threaten, coerce, and pass along messages. He seems to be orchestrating the entire legal defense, telling the girls which attorneys to hire and fire and ultimately convincing Susan Atkins to recant her statement. Fortunately, the prosecution has a second star witness to take her place: Linda Kasabian.

Part 5

Taking Linda Kasabian along on a ride to the crime scenes, Bugliosi extracts her story through tears of remorse. She says that at the Tate house, she saw Tex Watson shoot Steve Parent, but stayed in the car while the others went inside. She witnessed Patricia Krenwinkel chase Abigail Folger across the lawn and Tex Watson go after Voytek Frykowski before stabbing him repeatedly. Kasabian did not take part in the murders, but did not seek help because her daughter was still back at Spahn Ranch.

Recalling the night of the LaBianca murders, Kasabian supplies a wealth of information only one of the perpetrators could have known, including the location of Rosemary LaBianca's wallet. She fled the ranch in terror shortly after the crimes were committed.

Ballistics tests on spent bullet casings found at Spahn indicate that the same model of gun used in the Tate murders was used for target practice there. Going through the LAPD's evidence, Bugliosi finds a wooden door covered in graffiti, also taken from the ranch. The words "Helter Skelter" are printed on it.

Not permitted to represent himself in court, Manson chooses Irving Kanarek as his counsel. He's an attorney with a reputation for being disruptive in the courtroom and carrying on endless motions, dragging out simple cases for months. Manson causes his own disruptions, turning his back on the judge and striking a "crucifixion pose."

Part 6

The trial begins. Bugliosi explains that, even though Manson did not take part in the murders, he will be tried under the "vicarious liability" rule of conspiracy, which basically states that if he and his codefendants were all working toward the same conspiratorial goal (in this case, "helter skelter"), they are all equally guilty.

Manson appears in court with a bloody "X" carved into his forehead, claiming, "I have X'd myself from your world." His codefendants, and Mansonites on the outside, have "Xs" on their foreheads as well.

During Linda Kasabian's testimony, Manson is observed making a "slitting motion" with his finger across his throat. The antics crescendo when Manson grabs a pencil and leaps over the attorneys' table toward the judge, before being tackled by a bailiff.

SUMMARY AND ANALYSIS

Bugliosi gives his opening statement, laying out the "helter skelter" motive, and Linda Kasabian testifies. Irving Kanarek is found in contempt of court twice for his repeated interruptions. Testimony is given by experts regarding weapons, the state of the bodies, and the fingerprints. Danny DeCarlo testifies to Manson's use of the word "pig" and his theories about the impending race war.

Juan Flynn, a ranch hand from Spahn, provides similar testimony. He also recalls specifics about the night the LaBiancas were murdered, including Susan Atkins stating, "We're going to get some fucking pigs." Bugliosi loses his temper over Kanarek's behavior and receives his own contempt citation. Former Family member Brooks Poston testifies to his prior belief that Charles Manson was the second coming of Jesus Christ.

Steve "Clem" Grogan is let out on probation (from the auto theft charges of the Barker raid), despite warnings by Bugliosi's cocounsel that he is "exceedingly dangerous." Members of the Family begin loitering outside the courthouse, holding a "vigil." One member is quoted as saying, "I'm waiting for my father to get out of jail." Bugliosi is followed by Family members repeatedly and Manson himself threatens to kill Bugliosi, the judge, and his own attorney.

Prosecution witness and former Family member Barbara Hoyt is spirited away to Hawaii by the Family in an attempt to silence her. When it doesn't work, Manson follower Ruth Ann "Ouisch" Moorehouse slips ten tabs of LSD into Hoyt's hamburger, resulting in her hospitalization.

Tex Watson, awaiting trial, ceases speaking and eating and is placed in a mental hospital. Finally, in late November 1970, the prosecution rests, followed by the defense.

Part 7

Immediately after the defense rests, Atkins, Krenwinkel, and Van Houten demand to testify. They want to take all the responsibility for the murders. Manson is allowed to make a statement in closed court, without the presence of the jury. In a semi-coherent diatribe, he rails against the Vietnam War and the "system," professes his innocence, blames the Beatles, and declares his desire to beat everyone present to death with his microphone.

The following Monday, Van Houten's attorney Ronald Hughes fails to show up for court. He went camping over the weekend and disappeared. Many suspect he has been murdered by the Family because he was looking out for his client's best interests during the trial, laying all of the blame on Charlie.

Several Mansonites are charged in the drugging of Barbara Hoyt with conspiracy to prevent a witness from testifying; shockingly, they are let out on bail. Family members also try, and fail, to smuggle marijuana and a hacksaw into jail for Charles Manson.

In the guilt phase of the trial, the defense does a remarkably poor job. Leslie Van Houten's attorney insists that it is implausible that Manson would "send women to do a man's job"; Kanarek drones on for six consecutive days. Ultimately, the jury deliberates for nine days and reaches a verdict of guilty on all counts for all parties.

Part 8

The penalty phase of the trial begins. The girls' parents testify for the defense, pleading for their lives to be spared. Several Family members testify, including Catherine "Gypsy" Share, who makes the audacious claim that Linda Kasabian organized and ordered the murders as copycat crimes to the Gary Hinman murder so authorities would release Family member Bobby Beausoleil, who'd been charged with the killing of the music teacher. Susan Atkins testifies to the same, as well as her own total lack or remorse, calling the crimes "No big thing." Meanwhile, Tex Watson is released from the mental hospital.

Several doctors are called to attest to the girls' mental states and the possibility of LSD use as a mitigating factor in the crimes. They are in agreement that the girls are mentally competent, and possibly suffering from personality disorders, and that LSD could not have compelled them to commit murder.

Finally, the prosecution and defense make their pleas for the death penalty and life imprisonment, respectively. After two days of deliberations, the jury votes in favor of the death penalty for all four defendants. The body of attorney Ronald Hughes is found a few miles from where he had last been seen camping.

Epilogue

Tex Watson is convicted for his part in the Tate and LaBianca murders and given the death penalty. "Clem" Grogan, Manson, and another Family associate are convicted for the murders of Gary Hinman and Spahn Ranch hand Donald "Shorty" Shea, though the body of the latter had not yet been found. The sentence is death, but the judge commutes it to life imprisonment, remarking that Grogan was "too stupid" to know what he was doing.

Having hatched an outlandish plan to free Manson, several Family members, including Catherine "Gypsy" Share, rob a Los Angeles Western Surplus Store, collecting one hundred and forty guns before they are apprehended by police. One of Manson's disciples claims the group intended to hijack a plane and order their leader's release.

SUMMARY AND ANALYSIS

Many of Manson's major influences are outlined, including "The Process," a satanic cult operating in the late 1960s that preached the coming of a "violent Armageddon" and the return of Christ. Manson also repeatedly expressed admiration for Hitler in the presence of his followers.

Helter Skelter then goes through a roll call of unsolved murders that may have been committed by Manson and/or the Family. The body count is eleven, including attorney Ronald Hughes and the brother of a man believed to be Manson's father. In 1972, the California Supreme Court abolishes the death penalty, commuting all of the murderers' sentences to life imprisonment.

Afterword

The 1994 addendum marks the twenty-fifth anniversary of the murders. Here, Bugliosi reflects on the "most bizarre mass murder in the recorded annals of crime," Manson's continued status as a cult figure, and his prison experience so far, which includes an infraction for possessing contraband (a hot air balloon catalog) and being set on fire by a fellow inmate.

In 1975, Manson acolyte Lynette "Squeaky" Fromme attempted to assassinate Gerald Ford. She was given life imprisonment. Tex Watson is reportedly a born-again Christian, as is Susan Atkins. All of the murderers (with the exception of Manson) have expressed remorse for their crimes.

Timeline

July 27, 1969: Gary Hinman is murdered.

August 8, 1969: The Tate murders take place at 10050 Cielo Drive.

August 9, 1969: In the morning, the Polanskis' housekeeper finds the bodies at Cielo Drive. That night, the LaBianca murders take place.

August 16, 1969: Spahn Ranch is raided.

September 1, 1969: The gun used in the Tate murders is discovered by a child and turned over to police.

SUMMARY AND ANALYSIS

October 9–12, 1969: Barker Ranch is raided. Police arrest thirteen Family members, including Leslie Van Houten and Patricia Krenwinkel.

November 12–17, 1969: Motorcycle gang members Al Springer and Danny DeCarlo give statements about Charles Manson.

November 18, 1969: Bugliosi is assigned as prosecutor of the Tate and LaBianca cases.

November 30, 1969: Police match fingerprints at the Tate residence to Tex Watson and Patricia Krenwinkel.

December 5–8, 1969: A grand jury hears Susan Atkins's testimony and indicts the murderers.

June 15, 1970: The trial of Manson, Atkins, Van Houten, and Krenwinkel begins.

July 27–August 19, 1970: Linda Kasabian testifies.

November 16–19 1970: The prosecution and defense rest their cases.

January 15–25, 1971: The jury deliberates and returns with a verdict of guilty on all counts for Manson, Atkins, Van Houten, and Krenwinkel.

March 29, 1971: The jury returns with a death sentence for the murderers.

October 12–21, 1971: Tex Watson is convicted of seven counts of murder and given the death sentence.

August 21, 1971: Family members rob the Western Surplus Store.

February 18, 1972: The California Supreme Court abolishes the death penalty.

Cast of Characters

Susan Atkins: Member of the Manson Family who was present at the Hinman, Tate, and LaBianca murder scenes and admitted to stabbing Sharon Tate, though she later recanted. She was perhaps the most flamboyant of the "Manson Girls," brazenly bragging of her involvement in the murders to her cellmates and investigators. Atkins settled at Spahn Ranch with the Manson Family in 1967. She gave birth to a son, whom Manson named Zezozose Zadfrack Glutz. Known by her peers as Sadie Mae Glutz or Crazy Sadie, Susan Atkins was sentenced to life in prison.

Robert "Bobby" Beausoleil: Described as an attractive "young hippie musician," this member of the

SUMMARY AND ANALYSIS

Manson Family was guilty of stabbing Gary Hinman to death.

Danny DeCarlo: Member of the "Straight Satans" motorcycle gang, he was a friend of Charles Manson and lived with the Family for a few months at Spahn Ranch. He became concerned with all the "murder talk" and started to distance himself from the Mansonites.

Abigail Folger: Heir to the Folger Coffee fortune, Abigail graduated from Radcliffe College and worked in magazine publishing in New York City. At a bookstore party, she met Voytek Frykowski, with whom she moved to California in 1968. In Los Angeles, their relationship soured, and they were both using drugs frequently. Folger—along with Sharon Tate, Jay Sebring, and Frykowski—was murdered by Charles Manson's Family in Roman Polanski's house.

Wojiciech "Voytek" Frykowksi: A friend of Roman Polanski's, Frykowski was Folger's freeloading boyfriend.

William Garretson: Caretaker living in the guest house of 10050 Cielo Drive. His presence was undetected on the night of the murders and he was the only survivor on the scene.

Steve "Clem" Grogan: Manson associate and murderer with a history of insanity and a rap sheet that included indecent exposure, he was present at the LaBianca murder scene. Grogan was charged and convicted of killing Gary Hinman and Donald "Shorty" Shea.

Gary Hinman: Music teacher who was murdered at the age of thirty-four by Bobby Beausoleil. Bobby Beausoleil and Susan Atkins went to Hinman's house to steal money they believed he had inherited. When he protested, Beausoleil stabbed him to death.

Ronnie Howard: Fellow inmate of Susan Atkins in Dormitory 8000. Shocked by information Atkins shared with her about the crimes already committed by the Manson Family, Howard made it her mission to tell the police.

Barbara Hoyt: A former follower of Charles Manson and a witness for the prosecution, Hoyt began living with the Family at Spahn Ranch in 1969. She became suspicious when she saw some of the Family members watching the news about the Tate murders, and she later overheard Susan Atkins tell Ruth Ann Moorehouse that she had killed Sharon Tate. Hoyt, along with Sherry Cooper, another Family member, fled the ranch in Death Valley. Unsure about testifying at the trial, the Family sent Hoyt to Hawaii along with a couple other Manson girls. There, she was given food laced with LSD. Soon after, she collapsed and was rushed to the emergency room. She returned to California, and eagerly testified against the Family.

Ronald Hughes: Attorney for Leslie Van Houten suspected to have been murdered by the Family.

Irving Kanarek: Manson's attorney, a man with a reputation for longwinded speeches, stonewalling, and absurd objections that made the trial even more of a spectacle.

Linda Kasabian: Former Family member present at the Tate and LaBianca murders, Kasabian showed remorse over the murders and became a key witness for the prosecution. She moved to Spahn Ranch with her young daughter, Tanya, in 1969, and quickly became one of Manson's apprentices, believing that he could see her for who she really was. As the only Family member with a legal driving license, Kasabian drove the Family members to the commit the Tate murders and the LaBianca murders. Kasabian was the only Family member to express any sympathy for the victims, even suffering an emotional breakdown when she was brought back to the Tate house to reconstruct the crimes. More than any other testimony, it was Kasabian's that led to the convictions of Manson, Watson, Atkins, Krenwinkel, and Van Houten.

Patricia Krenwinkel: Disciple of Charles Manson, Patricia was present at the Tate and LaBianca murders; she was observed by Kasabian chasing a fleeing Abigail Folger across the lawn at the Tate house and stabbing her repeatedly.

Charles Manson: Born Charles Milles Maddox on November 12, 1934, Charles was the ringleader of the Manson Family cult. He is short in stature, and during his time as the leader of the Manson Family, he had shaggy dark hair and often wore buckskin clothing. Growing up, he spent time in and out of reform school and prison. He stole cars, passed stolen checks, committed burglaries and armed robberies, and was caught pimping.

Terry Melcher: Record producer and former occupant of 10050 Cielo Drive.

Ruth Ann "Ouisch" Moorehouse: Family member and attempted murderer of Barbara Hoyt.

Steve Parent: A recent high school graduate, Parent was hoping to sell a radio to William Garretson when he was murdered in his car.

SUMMARY AND ANALYSIS

Roman Polanski: A Polish director who was well known for his films *Cul-de-Sac* and *Rosemary's Baby* when he married the actress Sharon Tate.

Jay Sebring: A successful Hollywood hairdresser with his own salon and noteworthy clients including Frank Sinatra, Paul Newman, and Steve McQueen.

Catherine "Gypsy" Share: Family member involved in the attempt on Barbara Hoy's life. She was convicted of a lesser charge: "conspiracy to dissuade a witness from testifying."

Donald "Shorty" Shea: Hollywood stuntman and actor, Shea was murdered by the Manson Family. He worked as a ranch hand at Spahn Ranch before the Manson Family moved there. Shea's relationship quickly soured with Manson for various reasons: he was married to a black woman, which Manson considered despicable, and Shea was uncomfortable with the Manson Family's contempt for the law. In fact, he planned to help George Spahn remove the group from the ranch.

Al Springer: Member of the "Straight Satans" motorcycle gang, Springer heard Manson confess to involvement in the Tate murders. Twenty-six years old at the time of the murders, he was five foot nine, weighed one hundred and thirty pounds, and had a tidy and clean appearance. In fact, this was one of the reasons Springer didn't like the Manson Family, who he considered lived like "animals." When he went to Spahn Ranch to retrieve a friend and fellow "Straight Satan," Manson bragged to him about killing people and even invited Springer to stay and "enjoy" his women.

Despite having a fairly high IQ, he was illiterate. During a stint in prison from 1961 to 1967, he took guitar lessons from a fellow inmate. After his release, he made money panhandling. During the summer of 1967, he promoted himself as a spiritual teacher and guru in the Haight-Ashbury of San Francisco. He attracted many female followers, who would eventually become the Manson Family.

Ruthless, narcissistic, manipulative, and highly charismatic, Manson was a con man extraordinaire. Manson demanded absolute loyalty from his followers—spiritually, sexually, emotionally—and had convinced his followers he was the second coming of Christ. He orchestrated the Hinman and Tate-LaBianca murders.

Sharon Tate: Actress who met Polanski in 1966 on the set of his film *Eye of the Devil*. On January 20, 1968, she married Polanski, who directed and costarred with her in the film *The Fearless Vampire Killers*. Known for her beauty and considered a promising Hollywood newcomer, she was eight and a half months pregnant with her and Polanski's child at the time of her death.

Leslie "Sankston" Van Houten: Family member and murderer, present at the Tate and LaBianca murder scenes, she stabbed Rosemary LaBianca. Van Houten was introduced to Manson via Bobby Beausoleil and Catherine "Gypsy" Share. According to Barbara Hoyt, Van Houten was one of the female leaders of the group.

Paul Watkins: Former Family member and witness for the prosecution. Watkins joined the Manson Family in 1968, several months after leaving high school. He became Manson's "chief lieutenant." Attractive and only nineteen years old, one of his jobs was picking up girls for Charlie. Uneasy with Manson's eagerness to commit murder, he left the Family and became a witness for the prosecution, helping to explain Manson's belief in "helter skelter."

Charles "Tex" Watson: Family member and murderer who was present at the Tate and LaBianca murder scenes, he killed Jay Sebring, Steven Parent, Voytek Frykowski, and Leno LaBianca. Watson was Manson's right-hand man. According to Al Springer, Tex was the "brains" at the ranch, along with Charlie.

Upon his arrival at the Tate house, Watson said, "I am the Devil and I'm here to do the Devil's business."

In August 1969, Manson ordered Steve Grogan, Bruce Davis, and Tex Watson to kill Shea because Manson considered him a "snitch." The location of his body was not discovered until 1977, ten years after his death.

Direct Quotes and Analysis

"It was so quiet, one of the killers would later say, you could almost hear the sound of ice rattling in cocktail shakers in the homes way down the canyon."

This eerie statement sets an ominous tone for the start of the book. The quiet of the night was significant because several witnesses reported hearing screams and gunshots break the silence.

"He's going to be sitting there, looking at me, Manson is, isn't he?"

Danny DeCarlo is representative of all the witnesses when he professes fear at the idea of seeing Manson in court. Manson had bragged to many people, DeCarlo included, that he was a murderer, and frequently used threats and intimidation on his followers. Furthermore, it was becoming obvious to everyone that Manson was giving directives to the Family from prison, possibly even ordering the murder of Leslie Van Houten's attorney Ronald Hughes.

"You couldn't meet a nicer group of people."

In an interview with Sergeant Michael J. McGann, Family member Leslie Van Houten provides this extremely ironic statement describing the Manson Family. This demonstrates just how brainwashed Van Houten was, and how much she believed in Manson and the Family.

"I am the Devil and I'm here to do the Devil's business."

Family member Tex Watson allegedly said this to Voytek Frykowski before murdering him at Roman Polanski and Sharon Tate's house. In order to bring on "helter skelter" and start a race war, Manson directed Watson to kill those at the Tate house and blame it on the Black Panthers. Because they believed Armageddon was imminent in the form of a race war, the Family would do whatever it took to bring it on and protect themselves—including doing the "Devil's" work.

HELTER SKELTER

"You have to have a real love in your heart to do this for people."

Here, member of the Manson Family Susan Atkins explains to fellow inmate Virginia Graham why she stabbed Sharon Tate to death. This conversation occurred in November 1969, while Atkins was being held for murder. It is evidence of her psychosis that Atkins truly seemed to believe she was doing Sharon Tate a favor by murdering her.

"I lived with Charlie for one year straight and on and off for two years. I know Charlie. I know him inside and out. I became Charlie. Everything I once was, was Charlie. There was nothing left of me anymore. And all of the people in the Family, there's nothing left of them anymore, they're all Charlie too."

Former Family member Paul Watkins talking about what it was like to be a part of the Manson Family. Charlie was a master manipulator. He kept his followers in secluded locations, out of the reach of friends or family, controlling their access to food, drugs, and sex, and indoctrinating them constantly. He told them over and over that he was God and they were his followers until they believed they existed entirely and only in relation to him.

SUMMARY AND ANALYSIS

"Mr. and Mrs. America—you are wrong. I am not the King of the Jews nor am I a hippie cult leader. I am what you have made of me and the mad dog devil killer fiend leper is a reflection of your society."

A statement issued by Charles Manson after he was convicted for the Tate and LaBianca murders. Manson saw American society as corrupt and poisoned beyond rehabilitation, particularly because of unfettered capitalism, militarism, and racism—at least, this is what he espoused.

His whole "belief system" was likely invented to attract disaffected youth, and it worked well. For example, he claimed to be against bigotry, but he frequently used the N-word and his entire prophecy was predicated on "the blacks" being ill-equipped to effectively lead society. Manson was smart enough to parrot the standard countercultural narrative when it served him, but it's unlikely he believed much of it.

Trivia

1. President Nixon caused a splash during the trial when he commented on the glorification of Manson by the media, tacitly implying he believed Manson to be guilty. This led to the sequestered jury having to be transported in a van with soaped windows so they could not see any headlines as they rode to court.

2. Family member Lynnette "Squeaky" Fromme attempted to assassinate President Gerald Ford in Sacramento in 1975. She was sentenced to life in prison, but was paroled for "good conduct time" in 2009.

SUMMARY AND ANALYSIS

3. In 2009, filmmaker John Waters wrote a plea for Leslie Van Houten's release, calling her "a really good friend."

4. The Manson trial was the longest murder trial in American history at nine and a half months and the most expensive—until the O. J. Simpson trial—at $1 million.

5. Beach Boy Dennis Wilson was not a Family member, but he did know some of them. Members of the Family lived with him briefly, to the detriment of his wallet and sexual health. He initially admired Manson's music and introduced him to producer Terry Melcher.

6. The Family was communal in all aspects of their lives, sharing food, clothing, drugs, and even lovers. Children living on the ranch were raised communally and not permitted to spend too much time with their biological parents. This was another form of control for Manson, as the Family relied entirely on each other with no outside support system. They went along with it because they genuinely believed that Manson was Christ reincarnated and they were his devoted followers.

HELTER SKELTER

7. Charles Manson was inspired by the Beatles song "Helter Skelter." He interpreted the lyrics to describe "a war between whites and blacks that the Beatles were in favor of." In addition to referring to chaos, the term helter skelter also refers to a playground slide in the United Kingdom.

8. Charles Manson had many rules at Spahn Ranch. Books, watches, clocks, calendars, or prescription eyeglasses were not allowed on the ranch. Additionally, he never allowed the women to carry money. That way, if they ever left him, they would be penniless.

9. In addition to the dogma of cultish institutions like Scientology and "The Process," Manson reportedly drew inspiration from Dale Carnegie before he became a leader of the Family. In prison, Charles Manson took one of his leadership and self-improvement courses, offered as a way to help convicts adjust to the outside world. Manson studied his book *How to Win Friends and Influence People* and used the techniques to manipulate people when he was back on the outside.

10. While it is not known exactly how many children Manson fathered, thanks to the frequent group

SUMMARY AND ANALYSIS

orgies at the ranch, he does have at least three sons: two are named Charles Manson and the third Valentine, after Manson's favorite character in the science-fiction novel *Stranger in a Strange Land*, by Robert A. Heinlein.

What's That Word?

Admissible: Able to be allowed or considered in a legal case. Because codefendants cannot implicate one another in a trial, statements made by the perpetrators using the word "we" were not admissible.

Conjecture: The formation or expression of an opinion or theory without sufficient evidence for proof. The defense attorneys tried to argue that the "helter skelter" motive was conjecture.

Conspiracy: An agreement by two or more persons to commit a crime, fraud, or other wrongful act.

SUMMARY AND ANALYSIS

Corroborate: To make more certain; to confirm. It was important for Bugliosi's case that the defendants corroborated details from each others' statements.

Indictment: A formal accusation initiating a criminal case, presented by a grand jury and usually required for felonies and other serious crimes.

Implicate: To show to be also involved, usually in an incriminating manner.

Hearsay: Unverified, unofficial information gained or acquired from another and not part of one's direct knowledge.

Recant: To withdraw, disavow, or "take back" a statement, opinion, etc.

Sequestration: Segregation of others; isolation. Members of jury panels are often sequestered so they cannot not be influenced by learning about their case from newspapers or other media.

Critical Response

- A #1 *New York Times* bestseller
- An Edgar Award winner

"One of the best crime stories ever written."
—*Chicago Sun-Times*

"[A] social document of rare importance."
—*The New Republic*

"In the course of demystifying this bizarre and brutal case, Bugliosi is highly critical of . . . police performance . . . the press . . . the probation system . . . judges and attorneys and of individuals who have elevated Manson as a symbolic and even heroic figure."
—*Los Angeles Times*

SUMMARY AND ANALYSIS

"Everything else is in these pages: the interminable police work (much of it poor), and elaborate theory-building, the careful legal mechanics rewarded by the dramatic trials, the links of rock-n-roll to revolution (and Revelations), an endless collection of telling small details."
—*The New Republic*

"Perceptive, clearly written and fascinating . . . Bugliosi and Gentry have made Manson and his minions explicable in an eerie, compelling way."
—*The Boston Globe*

"The revelations in this book are incredible. The orgies, the willing murders, the callousness, the indifference are almost unbelievable . . . More fascinating than most fictional crime stories."
—*Manchester Union Leader*

"[In *Helter Skelter*'s] detailed, documented and annotated pages, in its description of the way in which the case was investigated and presented, in the background information it provides on the events and persons involved, in its recapitulation of mood and of the actions begging the scenes, it is arguably an indispensable contribution to the necessary dialogue."
—*Los Angeles Times*

About the Authors

Vincent Bugliosi was born in Hibbing, Minnesota, in 1934. He attended the University of Miami on a tennis scholarship, followed by law school at the University of California in Los Angeles. He received his law degree in 1964.

Just thirty-five years old when he was chosen to prosecute the Manson case, Bugliosi had been working at the Los Angeles County district attorney's office for five years. In the marathon-length trial, Bugliosi introduced 290 pieces of evidence and called eighty-four witnesses. He worked hundred-hour weeks, frequently sleeping on a cot in his office, and was assigned a bodyguard for his protection.

SUMMARY AND ANALYSIS

Inspired by the success of *Helter Skelter*, Bugliosi went on to publish more than a dozen books, including *Outrage: The Five Reasons Why O. J. Simpson Got Away with Murder*, and *Reclaiming History: The Assassination of President John F. Kennedy*. He was also known for his criticism of George W. Bush.

Bugliosi passed away in 2015 at age eighty after a battle with cancer.

Curt Gentry was born in Lamar, Colorado, and worked as a journalist before joining the Air Force during the Korean War. He graduated from San Francisco State College and wrote extensively about California history before teaming up with Bugliosi to cowrite *Helter Skelter*. He also published an exhaustively researched and well-received biography of J. Edgar Hoover. He passed away in 2014.

For Your Information

Online
"Little-Known Facts About the Manson Murders." CNN.com
"The Manson Family and the Gruesome Murder of Sharon Tate." TheLineup.com
"The Manson Family on Trial: Madness Visible." Time.com
"Murderer, Love & Redemption." OrangeCoast.com
"Q&A: Manson Prosecutor Vincent Bugliosi." Time.com
"What Did Charles Manson Hear in the Music of the Beatles?" TheLineup.com
"Where are they now? Charles Manson's family, four decades after horrific murder spree." LATimes.com

SUMMARY AND ANALYSIS

Books

Coroner by Thomas Noguchi and Joseph DiMona

A Death in Canaan: A Classic Case of Good and Evil in a Small New England Town by Joan Barthel

Female Serial Killers: How and Why Women Become Monsters by Peter Vronsky

In Cold Blood by Truman Capote

Manson: The Life and Times of Charles Manson by Jeff Guinn

Sharon Tate and the Manson Murders by Greg King

The Stranger Beside Me by Ann Rule

Select Books by Vincent Bugliosi

Drugs in America: The Case for Victory: A Citizen's Call to Action

Four Days in November: The Assassination of President John F. Kennedy

No Island of Sanity: Paula Jones v. Bill Clinton: The Supreme Court on Trial

Outrage: The Five Reasons Why O. J. Simpson Got Away with Murder

The Phoenix Solution: Getting Serious about Winning America's Drug War

The Prosecution of George W. Bush for Murder

Reclaiming History: The Assassination of President John F. Kennedy

Bibliography

Associated Press. "'Squeaky' Fromme Released from Prison." NBCNews.com, August 14, 2009. http://www.nbcnews.com/id/32416452/ns/us_news-crime_and_courts/t/squeaky-fromme-released-prison/#.V_fxkPkrLIU.

Bugliosi, Vincent and Curt Gentry. *Helter Skelter*. New York: W.W. Norton & Company, 1974.

"Charles Manson: Master Manipulator, Even as a Child." NPR.org, August 4, 2013. http://www.npr.org/2013/08/04/206652873/charles-manson-master-manipulator-even-as-a-child.

Garber-Paul, Elizabeth. "Manson Family: Where Are They Now?" *Rolling Stone*, July 27, 2016. http://www.rollingstone.com/culture/pictures/manson-family-where-are-they-now-w430665/clem-grogan-w430674.

Huffington Post. "Vincent Bugliosi." HuffingtonPost.com, accessed on September 30, 2016. http://www.huffingtonpost.com/author/vincent-bugliosi.

"Jonestown," History.com, accessed on November 1, 2016. http://www.history.com/topics/jonestown.

Kirsch, Robert. Review of *Helter Skelter*, by Vincent Bugliosi. *Los Angeles Times*, accessed on October 9, 2016. http://www.latimes.com/books/jacketcopy/la-et-jc-helter-skelter-by-vincent-bugliosi-the-1974-book-review-20150609-story.html.

Stout, David. "Vincent T. Bugliosi, Manson Prosecutor and True-Crime Author, Dies at 80." *New York Times*, June 9, 2015. http://www.nytimes.com/2015/06/10/us/vincent-t-bugliosi-manson-prosecutor-and-true-crime-author-dies-at-80.html?_r=0.

Trounson, Rebecca and Elaine Woo. "Famed Manson Family Prosecutor Vincent Bugliosi dies at 80." *Los Angeles Times*, June 9, 2015. http://www.latimes.com/local/obituaries/la-me-vincent-bugliosi-20150609-story.html.

Waters, John. "Leslie Van Houten: A Friendship." *Huffington Post*, September 3, 2009. http://www.huffingtonpost.com/john-waters/leslie-van-houten-a-frien_b_246953.html.

Woods, William Crawford. "Demon in the Counterculture." *The New Republic*, January 4, 1975. https://newrepublic.com/article/114233/stacks-charles-manson-helter-skelter-and-counterculture.

Yardley, William. "Curt Gentry, 83, Co-Author of 'Helter Skelter,' Dies," *New York Times*, July 20, 2014. http://www.nytimes.com/2014/07/21/books/curt-gentry-83-co-author-of-helter-skelter-dies.html.

WORTH BOOKS
SMART SUMMARIES

So much to read, so little time?

Explore summaries of bestselling fiction and essential nonfiction books on a variety of subjects, including business, history, science, lifestyle, and much more.

Visit the store at
www.ebookstore.worthbooks.com

MORE SMART SUMMARIES
FROM WORTH BOOKS

TRUE CRIME

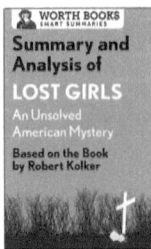

Find a full list of our authors and
titles at www.openroadmedia.com

FOLLOW US
@OpenRoadMedia

www.ingramcontent.com/pod-product-compliance
Lightning Source LLC
Chambersburg PA
CBHW060342080526
44584CB00013B/884